SOLAR ENERGY

PUTTING THE SUN TO WORK

JESSIE ALKIRE

Consulting Editor, Diane Craig, M.A./Reading Specialist

Super Sandcastle

An Imprint of Abdo Publishing
abdopublishing.com

abdopublishing.com

Published by Abdo Publishing, a division of ABDO, PO Box 398166, Minneapolis, Minnesota 55439. Copyright © 2019 by Abdo Consulting Group, Inc. International copyrights reserved in all countries. No part of this book may be reproduced in any form without written permission from the publisher. Super SandCastle™ is a trademark and logo of Abdo Publishing.

Printed in the United States of America, North Mankato, Minnesota

052018
092018

Design and Production: Mighty Media, Inc.
Editor: Megan Borgert-Spaniol
Cover Photographs: Shutterstock; Wikimedia Commons
Interior Photographs: Alamy; Bnc319/Wikimedia Commons; Shutterstock; Wikimedia Commons

Library of Congress Control Number: 2017961857

Publisher's Cataloging-in-Publication Data
Names: Alkire, Jessie, author.
Title: Solar energy: Putting the sun to work / by Jessie Alkire.
Other titles: Putting the sun to work
Description: Minneapolis, Minnesota : Abdo Publishing, 2019. | Series: Earth's
    energy innovations
Identifiers: ISBN 9781532115745 (lib.bdg.) | ISBN 9781532156465 (ebook)
Subjects: LCSH: Solar energy--Juvenile literature. | Power resources--Juvenile
    literature. | Energy development--Juvenile literature. | Energy conversion--
    Juvenile literature.
Classification: DDC 621.47--dc23

Super SandCastle™ books are created by a team of professional educators, reading specialists, and content developers around five essential components—phonemic awareness, phonics, vocabulary, text comprehension, and fluency—to assist young readers as they develop reading skills and strategies and increase their general knowledge. All books are written, reviewed, and leveled for guided reading, early reading intervention, and Accelerated Reader™ programs for use in shared, guided, and independent reading and writing activities to support a balanced approach to literacy instruction.

CONTENTS

What Is Solar Energy?   4

Energy Timeline   6

Fire and Heat   8

Modern Solar Heat   10

Solar Cells   12

Heat and Electricity   14

Solar Collectors   16

Solar Panels   18

Shining Forward   20

More About Solar Energy   22

Test Your Knowledge   23

Glossary   24

WHAT IS SOLAR ENERGY?

Solar panels

Solar energy is energy created by sunlight. It can be used for heat and electricity. People use **solar panels** to power buildings. The panels turn sunlight into electricity.

Solar energy is a clean energy. It does not pollute the air. But making solar panels does create waste and pollution.

Solar energy is renewable. Sunlight won't run out for millions of years!

ENERGY TIMELINE

200s BCE

Greeks and Romans use the sun's energy to burn torches.

1200s CE

The Anasazi build homes in cliffs facing the sun. This keeps the homes warm during winter.

1767

Horace de Saussure invents an early form of solar oven.

Discover how solar energy has changed over time!

1948

Mária Telkes **designs** the first modern solar-heated home.

1954

US scientists create the first **solar cell**. They use it to power an electric toy.

2017

US company Tesla begins selling solar roof tiles.

FIRE AND HEAT

People have used solar energy for thousands of years. In the 200s BCE, Greeks and Romans used mirrors to direct sunlight. This produced flames to light torches.

In the 1200s CE, Anasazi Native Americans used the sun's heat. They built dwellings in cliffs facing the sun. This kept them warm during winter.

Greeks lit torches for ancient Olympic Games.

Anasazi cliff dwellings at Mesa Verde National Park in Colorado

MODERN SOLAR HEAT

Researchers later experimented with solar energy. In 1767, Swiss scientist Horace de Saussure created a solar collector. This was a special box that trapped heat from the sun. It was an early form of solar oven.

Horace de Saussure

Scientists continued to study solar energy. Hungarian-American Mária Telkes was one of them. She designed the first modern solar-heated home in 1948.

MÁRIA TELKES

BORN: December 12, 1900,
Budapest, Hungary

DIED: December 2, 1995,
Budapest, Hungary

Mária Telkes was a solar
scientist. She invented the first
solar **distiller**. This device uses
the sun's heat to purify water.
Telkes also designed the first
modern solar-heated home. It
used solar collectors to capture
heat. Telkes received many
awards for her work!

SOLAR CELLS

Solar cell

Soon after, **researchers** used solar energy to power electronics. In 1954, US scientists created the first **solar cell**. The cell was made of **silicon**. It could power a small toy Ferris wheel!

Scientists have continued to study solar cells. Solar cells are also called photovoltaic cells. They are used in many devices. Solar cells power wristwatches and cars. They even power **satellites** in space!

The International Space Station is a satellite. More than 200,000 solar cells power the station!

HEAT AND ELECTRICITY

One use of solar energy is heat. Solar energy can heat homes and businesses. The heat can be used immediately or stored for later.

Another use of solar energy is electricity. Solar energy can power streetlights. It can also power homes. Scientists think solar energy could power entire cities. It could even power the whole world!

Solar-powered streetlights

Power lines transmit electricity from solar power plants to consumers.

SOLAR COLLECTORS

Solar collectors

Solar collectors capture solar energy to produce heat. These devices are often set up on roofs. Sunlight heats a collector. The heat is sent through air or water. The heat can be stored or used right away.

Concentrated collectors produce more heat. They direct sunlight with mirrors. This increases the light's strength. These collectors can produce very high temperatures. They are commonly used in solar power plants.

The Ivanpah concentrated solar power plant is in California.
It uses thousands of mirrors to direct sunlight at power towers.

SOLAR PANELS

Silicon

Solar power is produced by **solar panels**. These devices are made up of many **solar cells**. The cells are made of metal and **silicon**. Sunlight strikes the point where these parts meet. This creates electricity.

One solar cell creates about 2 **watts** of power. That is enough to power two small light bulbs. A solar panel can produce hundreds of watts of power!

Like solar collectors, solar panels are set up on roofs. They are used to power homes and businesses.

SHINING FORWARD

Tesla solar roof tiles

Solar energy is a popular **resource** today. In 2017, US company Tesla began selling solar roof tiles. These tiles work like **solar panels** but look like regular roof tiles.

Solar tiles and panels are costly. More people could afford solar power if costs go down. Solar power may soon be a main energy resource!

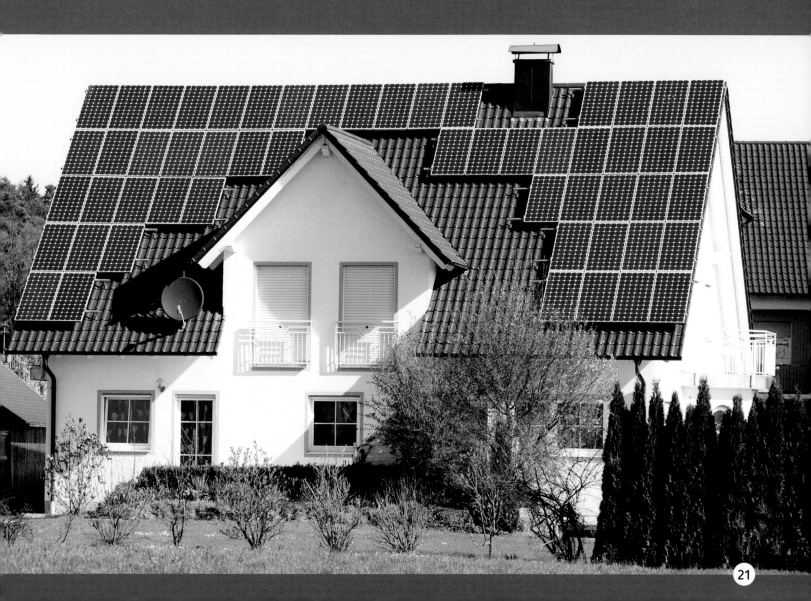

Solar panel systems store electricity for times when sunlight is low.

MORE ABOUT SOLAR ENERGY

Do you want to tell others about solar energy? Here are some fun facts to share!

IN 2013, US President Barack Obama had **solar panels** put in at the White House.

THE AMOUNT OF SUNLIGHT that hits Earth in one hour could power the world for more than a year!

IN 2016, *Solar Impulse 2* became the first solar-powered airplane to fly around the world.

TEST YOUR KNOWLEDGE

1. Solar energy is a clean energy. **TRUE OR FALSE?**

2. In what year did Mária Telkes **design** a solar-heated home?

3. What is another name for a **solar cell**?

THINK ABOUT IT!

Have you seen **solar panels** on a roof? What did they look like?

ANSWERS: 1. True 2. 1948 3. Photovoltaic cell

23

GLOSSARY

concentrate – to direct or focus something.

design – to plan how something will appear or work.

distiller – a device that makes a liquid or other substance pure by heating and cooling it.

researcher – someone who tries to find out more about something.

resource – something that is usable or valuable.

satellite – a manufactured object that orbits Earth.

silicon – the second most common element in Earth's crust. It is used in computers and other electronics.

solar cell – a device that converts sunlight into electricity.

solar panel – a large, flat surface made up of many solar cells.

watt – a unit of electric power.